50 WAYS TO SAVE THE

HONEY BEES

(AND CHANGE THE WORLD)

50 WAYS TO SAVE THE HONEY BEES

(AND CHANGE THE WORLD)

BY J. SCOTT DONAHUE

CIDER MILL
PRESS

BOOK
PUBLISHERS

Kennebunkport, ME

13-Digit ISBN: 978-1604336481
10-Digit ISBN: 160433648X

This book may be ordered by mail from the publisher. Please include $5.95 for postage and handling. Please support your local bookseller first!

Books published by Cider Mill Press Book Publishers are available at special discounts for bulk purchases in the United States by corporations, institutions, and other organizations. For more information, please contact the publisher.

Cider Mill Press Book Publishers
"Where good books are ready for press"

PO Box 454
12 Spring Street
Kennebunkport, Maine 04046
Visit us on the Web! www.cidermillpress.com

Cover design by Alicia Freile, Tango Media
Interior design by Alicia Freile, Tango Media
Typography: Amatic, Birka, Bodoni and Gotham
All images are used under official license from Shutterstock.
See p. 158 for more details.

Printed in China
1 2 3 4 5 6 7 8 9 0
First Edition

TABLE OF CONTENTS

For the wild places and people

The State of Our Hives

Ever wonder how the world achieves its springtime luminosity and succor? Well, from dawn 'til dusk, a swarm of workers each cover two to five miles from bud to bud, blossom to blossom, apple to apple. They labor in mid-air, performing nature's heavy lifting by carrying cargo loads of pollen and nectar. And the fruits of their labor are these: bountiful harvests, verdant landscapes, and a ripe global agriculture industry worth hundreds of billions of dollars a year.

So what happens when the work suddenly halts? What does the world look like if hundreds of millions of these workers—our amazing honey bees—just disappear off the face of the Earth?

When honey bees stop working, they die. Due to a widespread variety of diseases sweeping through honey bee colonies, bees across the planet are vanishing at unsustainable numbers. **Colony Collapse Disorder**, or **CCD**, is one of the most startling culprits of this complicated phenomenon. CCD occurs when worker bees, by the thousands, buzz off and abandon a hive—like factory workers on strike. As a result, the economy of the colony slows to a halt. Honeycomb quotas are left unmet. Flowers and fruits shrivel and forgo their reproduction. And the entire enterprise of the hive— the succession of a new Queen, the building up of food stores and rearing the next brood of workers—goes out of business.

Apiologists—scientists who study bees—began noticing the grave trend in nihilistic behavior among worker bees in 2006. What was widely accepted before as a phenomenon called "Autumn Collapse" now became something worse: A baffling 30% of North America's honey bee population ceased to exist by winter of that year. Since then, CCD decimates close to one third of colony populations *per year* in North America.

The plight of honey bees is not confined to North America either. The discovery of CCD in 2006 set the global scientific community abuzz as apiologists from around the world began to observe a similar phenomenon. Bee biologists scratched their heads over colonies shuttering at such alarming rates similar to those in the States. Today, Russia, United Kingdom, China, India—and wherever any economy depends on bees for agriculture—are bearing the brunt of diminishing bee populations. After all, bees generate $200 billion dollars *annually* in global industry. That's more than the combined net worth the world's two richest men, Bill Gates and Carlos Slim, make in one year!

The crisis of CCD fills us with an overwhelming need to answer the question, "Why is this happening?" If only the answer were as ready as a solution to a campy disaster movie (think M. Night Shyamalan's *The Happening*). There is simply no smoking-gun cause for collapsing colonies, and a global population hitting nine billion souls by 2050 will put added stress on our demands for food and materials brought to us by bees. Apiologists have discovered a mélange of natural and man-made problems, however, that could be to blame for CCD. Pesticides, changing climate, microbes and parasites are some of myriad stressors on bee populations.

A world without honey bees means a world without fruits, vegetables, flowers and raw goods. A world without bees is a world desaturated of sweetness and vibrancy.

The truth stings—but there's hope. This book will give you the skills and savvy to save bees—simply by using a ballot, spade or wallet. We can save the honey bee by the way we garden, buy food, donate our time and take up hobbies. Most of all, we can model ourselves after resourcefulness and industriousness of the honey bee, putting our every waking hour into a sustainable future.

FROM "THE GEORGICS" BY VIRGIL, BOOK IV

When the golden sun has driven winter back down
Under the earth and opened up the sky
With the radiance of summer, then the bees
Fly everywhere through all the groves and glades,
Gathering from the beautiful flowers and lightly
Imbibing from the surface of the streams.
It's thus that, motivated by some joy
I know not how to name, they go about
The caring for their offspring and their nests;
It's thus that artfully they make new wax
And shape and form and mold their clinging honey.
And so, when you look up and see the swarm,
Emancipated from the hive and floating
Up to the starry sky through the summer air,
Or when you wonder at the sight of a dark
Cloud carried along and drifting on the wind,
Take heed, for there they are, on the hunt for leafy
Shelter near sweet water...

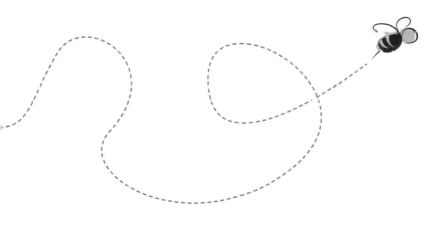

Anatomy of a Colony

Imagine a kingdom that fits inside of a box no bigger than a newspaper vending machine. Inside this box: A Queen commands close to 80,000 of her loyal subjects to clean, cook, forage and—if worthy enough—mate with the monarch herself. Every single member of the kingdom lives and dies in servitude to keep the hive alive for generations.

Such are the inner workings of a honey bee colony, a caste system of various bees naturally selected for a task. Any fundamental change in the behavior of drones, workers or a Queen collapses a colony.

QUEEN: 1 PER COLONY

Every honey bee depends upon the **Queen**—the only fertile female bee who spends her life laying eggs and giving out orders with her irresistible pheromones. This domestic goddess sports a long, slender body that shines with a royal coat. She births between 20,000 and 80,000 female worker bees and 1,000 male drones. Many more future queens will also pupate, but only a rightful ruler can survive to command the hive.

WORKERS: 20,000 TO 80,000 PER COLONY

Workers are the Queen's little minions. Their chores range from the domestic—cleaning the nest, feeding larvae and caring for the Queen—to the adventurous, scouting for new sources of pollen and defending the hive. And at the start of the day, workers instruct other workers of the hive with a special **waggle dance**—a dance that communicates where the sweet spots are to pollinate, and how far. Because of their vast numbers, workers are the most vulnerable to Colony Collapse triggers: cold snaps, heat exhaustion, over-crowding, deadly chemicals and diseases within the colony. Workers really pack a wallop in their stinger. They engage in combat when defending the hive from external threats. A worker can fly up to five miles in one day's work and carry nearly half her weight in nectar. And with daily contact with gardens or farms, workers can carry back to their hives harmful pesticides, parasites or diseases that ransack a colony.

Along with many other responsibilities, worker bees also execute weak workers that underperform their tasks in the hive, or even drones that fail their big chance with the queen. Perhaps getting fired isn't so bad after all!

DRONES: 1,000 PER COLONY

Drones, bulky and male, are larger and stronger than worker honey bees, though not as strong as the Queen. However, they don't perform the macho work of fighting like the workers do. Drones spend their entire existence waiting for one moment: a mating flight with the Queen, also called a **swarm.** During the swarm, thousands of bulky drones race each other to catch the Queen suspended in flight, impregnate the Queen, and then drop dead from the ecstasy and exhaustion.

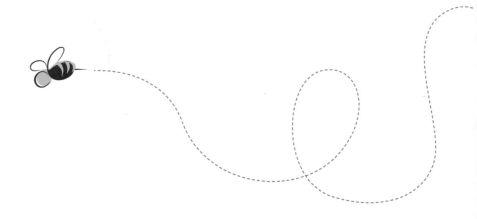

THE BODY OF THE HONEY BEE:

Six legs, a head, abdomen and thorax. Though the sting is the most well-known feature, honey bees also have nectar pouches inside their bodies and a long proboscis to draw in nectar, water and honey.

CHAPTER TWO

Gardening to Sustain Bee Colonies

A worker bee begins her day scouting out the most plentiful sources to collect the choicest pollen and nectar. She sees flowers the way we see neon signs, and is caught in an electromagnetic tango with a flower stamen. After finding her plum source of pollen or nectar, the worker reports back to the hive to perform her waggle dance, instructing her co-workers where to fly, and how far.

The flowers in our pots, the cherry tomatoes on our windowsill and the summer squash in our community gardens all have a dependency on being found by bees. And bees require the most attractive and nutritious flora to thrive. Which flowers, fruits and veggies do bees love most? The answer could fill a book much longer than this! Instead, a better approach is this: Which flowers, fruits and veggies *love bees* the most? Since so much depends upon climate, here are the best choices for each quarter trip around the sun. And the flowers, fruits and vegetables that belong to you and your neighbor will thank you.

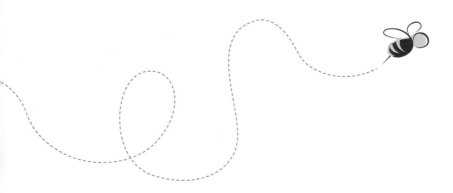

Bees have a hivemind for mathematics. Honeycomb is shaped like a hexagon to minimize surface area within a hive.

1

PLANT FOR THE FORAGE.

Beekeepers have 101 ways to feed their bees—most of them being artificial, containing a mixture of sugar and water. When it comes to the best source of nutrition for honey bees, however, nothing rivals the buds and blooms. Grow the plants, fruits and herbs bees that love. Grow natively. Grow seasonally. Build a bee's "Garden of Earthly Delights."

PLANT IN THE SPRINGTIME:

Love is in the air, and so are flower gametes! Bees and other pollinators (along with the wind) take responsibility for the reproduction of our lush planet. Honey bees usher in the spring season with a booming brood of healthy workers to do nature's every bidding, and a flourishing hive during this season means prolific activity. The thawing of winter, gentle weather and longer hours of daylight give the honey bees the best conditions and even better sensory perception of flowers.

FLOWERS THAT BLOOM: pale purple coneflowers, common yarrows, lilacs, pink lilies
FRUITS THAT GROW: strawberries, peaches
VEGETABLES THAT SPROUT: cucumbers, onions, legumes

3 PLANT IN THE SUMMER:

The busiest time of year for the bee means long days, hot temperatures and dropping populations of worker bees. In fact, one third of worker bees only last six weeks during the summer; they work themselves to death! Meanwhile, the Queen takes her mating flight with hot-and-bothered drones in pursuit. And soon, the summer cycle continues as a new brood of workers is born.

FLOWERS: sunflowers, sweet williams, foxgloves, crocuses
FRUITS: watermelons, kiwifruits, plums, cantaloupes
VEGETABLES: okras, celery, beets

If you want to find the sweetest watermelon of the bunch, look for the bee kisses—little brown blemishes on the melon's green rind. The more bee kisses, the more succulent a watermelon tastes!

4

PLANT IN AUTUMN:

Shakespeare, who understood the seasonal plight of the honey bee, once wrote of this season: *"That time of year thou may'st in me bee-hold."* The fall marks a time when bees' production begins to slow, days become shorter and temperatures begin to drop. As bees struggle to fulfill their purpose, the world begins its long exhale. Leaves turn, flowers wither, fruits break off their stems in a gust of wind.

FLOWERS: bergamot, poppies, echinops, hellebores
FRUITS: Himalayan blackberries, clementines, pomegranates, raspberries
VEGETABLES: heirloom tomatoes, butternut squash, potatoes

5 PLANT IN WINTER:

Winter is the cruelest season for bees. During this month, up to half of the worker population dies off simply from lack of work, while others survive the winter cold in hibernation. While bees form a vibrating winter cluster to keep warm, beekeepers strategize against the coldest months by planting year-round flora for bees to keep busy.

FLOWERS: primulas, clematis, mignonettes
FRUITS: oranges, tangerines, apples, blackberries, persimmon, Asian pear
VEGETABLES: squash, cauliflower, broccoli, carrots

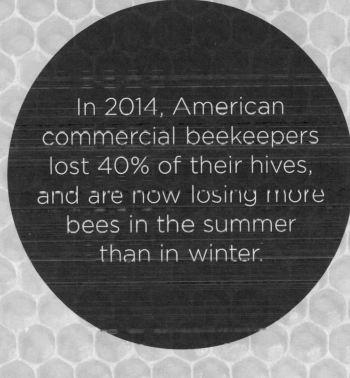

In 2014, American commercial beekeepers lost 40% of their hives, and are now losing more bees in the summer than in winter.

6

FAMILIARIZE YOURSELF WITH LOCAL FLORA.

Beekeepers, as you will find, are also part-time botanists. They know—particularly by the color of the honey their bees produce—which flowers and fruits their bees have visited. And a colony depends on beekeepers to understand how to raise healthy, bee-friendly plants.

7 AVOID PESTICIDES

namely **neonicotinoids**. These pesticide components—"neonics" for short—shut down the nerve systems of insects, including honey bees. Chemically similar to nicotine, these harmful toxins have been the bane of beekeepers' existence. More than 30 scientific studies have been published, showing a link between neonicotinoids and colony collapse.

8

WELCOME LADYBUGS, SPIDERS AND PRAYING MANTISES

to your garden. These bugs serve as sentries to a garden, and offer a clean alternative to harmful pesticides.

9 RETHINK THE LAWN ENTIRELY.

Lawn culture, especially in California where a four-year drought weighs heavily on the minds of suburban agriculturalists, is passé. However, unkempt lawns can be a paradise for honey bees, who love dandelions, clovers and other weeds. If you aren't ready to trade your sod for a rock garden, then instead give a patch of lawn the *au natural* treatment and see what the soil grows and attracts on its own.

10

DON'T HANG YELLOW JACKET TRAPS in your yard. These bright yellow snares that hang from trees kill our vital honey bees and other pollinators unnecessarily.

11

AVOID HYBRIDIZED PLANTS.

Plants hybridized for their size and color tend to benefit florists over bees, and only produce scant amounts of nectar and pollen compared to robust, heirloom plants.

12

CREATE A "BEE BATH."

Bee baths are crucial during the summer months, when workers begin to die off from exhaustion. Construct a bee bath simply by filling a shallow basin with water and making a small "island" of pebbles or gravel for bees to perch safely and take in water.

A hive of honey bees will fly a total of 90,000 miles in a generation. That's three trips around the earth.

KEEPING TO SUSTAIN HONEY BEES

ees have been treated as livestock for millennia. We depend
on bees, and in turn honey bees—namely the Western honey
bee (*Apis mellifera*)—have now (for better or worse) become
dependent on us to keep them healthy. We've created a symbiotic
relationship with honey bees, and with this relationship we've also
brought myriad health problems for bees too. While we depend on
honey bees to pollinate our crops, honey bees in turn depend on us
to keep them free of diseases spread by commercialized honey that
transport bees from farm to farm, and invasive species that resulted
from our global enterprising of the honey bee.

Although large-scale beekeeping has contributed to the proliferation of illnesses and pests in honey bees, small-scale beekeeping—in backyards or on rooftops—can be seen as a remedy. Now that we understand the inner workings of the colony, along with the forage bees prefer throughout the seasons, we can take steps to raise our own bees. Here are some of the ways we as beekeepers can help keep them healthy and thriving.

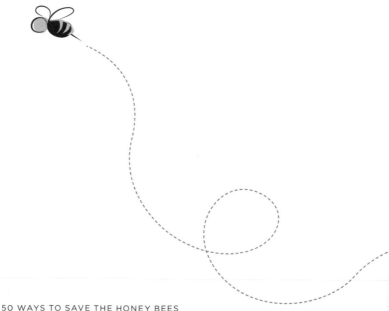

Field Notes:
A bee's reason to BEE

What drives the worker bee to buzz? After all, she doesn't work for us. She doesn't work for the US agriculture industry, even though she pulls in $15 billion a year in profits. She doesn't work for the sake of the charismatic Queen. In turn, the Queen doesn't live for the sake of her adoring workers. And drones, who spend their entire existence preparing for a rendezvous with the Queen, don't race each other to near death just for bragging rights. What is their raison d'etre; what could be their reason to *bee*? A bee's brain is only a cluster of tangled proteins, yet a hive of bees becomes a single organism with one humming consensus of a purpose: the future. Their role is to pass on their enterprise to the next generation of drones, workers and a new queen.

13 JOIN THE COMMUNITY.

Beekeepers are a brilliant group of individuals who think and work collectively as a hive; similar to the way bees exist as a hive, beekeepers thrive off of each other's work, anecdotes and directions. Shadowing a honey harvest is a great way to dip your feet into beekeeping without going the whole nine yards of buying equipment.

Joining a beekeeping community also means taking part in a tradition that is thousands of years old. In fact, the earliest record of a beekeeper appears on a limestone cave painting in Spain's Araña Caves, dating back to 6,000 B.C.

The cave painting depicts a figure with what could be a smoking stick in one hand and bag slung over the shoulder. The image of the earliest beekeeper known to ascend a tree to retrieve a few slabs of honeycomb—defensive bees buzzing about the head—proves just how old our infatuation with honey foraging is.

Volumes upon volumes have been written about beekeeping. The classical poet Virgil crafted instructional verse to other beekeepers, even describing the diseases we still see today in beehives. The most important acquisition for any aspiring beekeeper is a library card.

14

GET YOUR HANDS STICKY.

It's about taking a hands-on learning approach with beekeeping. **Apiaries**—a space for bees to be kept—are outdoor labs for the beekeeper. By shadowing a beekeeper, you'll not only learn the intricate ins and outs of a beehive, but you'll also get an idea if beekeeping is your cup of nectar. Every beekeeper starts as an amateur; finding a mentor, making friends and really getting your hands covered in honey will ease any apprehensions or anxiety you may feel when committing to the hobby of beekeeping.

15 ACQUIRE THE EQUIPMENT.

A movement in sustainable beekeeping, also called "Treatment Free Beekeeping," gained traction after 2006 when Colony Collapse Disorder made international news, and neonicotinoids and other treatment chemicals appeared to be culpable. As more and more amateur beekeepers began to raise bees to combat the sharp decline of pollinators, treatment-free equipment for small-scale beekeepers became a must.

Here is a checklist of the supplies you will need, courtesy of beekeepers Rob and Chelsea MacFarland, founders of HoneyLove.org and authors of *Save the Bees with Natural Backyard Hives:*

- Hivewire:
    - Hive boxes, $25 each
    - Bottom board, $15
    - Top board, $15
    - Frames, $3
- Weatherproofing, $20
- Starter strips, $10
- Protective Clothing:
    - Suit, $100
    - Veil, $35
    - Gloves, $25
- Smoker, $25
- Hive tool, $15
- Savvy
- Patience

SAVE THE BEES WITH NATURAL BACKYARD HIVES, by Rob and Chelsea McFarland

16

BUY A QUEEN; RAISE A COLONY.

After investing in the hive boxes and equipment (and overcoming the confusion of how to put what where), the next venture into beekeeping begins with the purchase of a Queen. Some beekeeping supply companies will isolate queens and sell them individually through beekeeping stores. Packaged queens can even be shipped to your front door from an online or over-the-phone purchase.

Whole bee colonies (called nucleus or "nuc" colonies) can come in packages as well, weighing up to three pounds.

17 CATCH A SWARM.

When honey bees swarm, the workers look for a new nest while the Queen and drones are in the throes of mating season. A Queen bee jettisons from her post into the summer air while drones chase her and protective workers—the vast majority of bees in the swarm—escort the hive. Only the fastest- and strongest-flying male drones get a shot at mating with the queen—and afterwards the drones plop to the ground, their life's purpose fulfilled and their strong genes passed on. Catching bees in a swarm promises for a fully stocked hive come springtime.

Swarms will appear like a great ball of bees, humming on a branch of a tree or arm of a saguaro cactus. To catch a swarm, you will need a box or bucket (along with a suit, gloves and veil). If they've taken to a branch, knock it with a stick to get the swarm into the box or bucket. Once the queen lands inside, the rest of the hive will follow her and stay put.

18

CATCH FERAL BEES.

Honey bees can be a little too close for comfort at times, especially when tens of thousands of honey bees decide to roost in a tree by a jungle gym. Rather than calling pest control or attempting to exterminate the bees (definitely don't do that), call a beekeeper to assist him or her in safely procuring the feral bees.

19

REUSE BEE INFRASTRUCTURE: WAX, FRAMES AND REPURPOSED BOXES.

Bee cells and wax can be reused and repurposed by bees for their necessities. When harvesting honey, be courteous enough to leave an inch or two of wax around the frame's edges.

20

BUILD YOUR OWN HIVE BOXES FOR THE BEES.

If you have the woodshop know-how, building your own bee boxes can be a fun foray into the business aspect of beekeeping.

21

VISIT LOCAL BEEKEEPERS

Ever dipped your finger in honey straight from the hive? Visit a beekeeper to don the safety apparel and get a hands-on understanding of how to raise bees and enjoy their gifts.

22 KNOW THE ENEMY: PATHOGENS AND PESTS.

Beekeeping demands a knowledge for the pests and pathogens that are known to kill bees in unsustainable numbers. Some of the most common that clear out a hive:

CHALKBROOD is a fungus that invades a hive and attacks vulnerable, new broods of larvae.

Symptoms: Larvae will turn ghost white and fill up with cotton-like spores, leaving behind a petrified husk.

Prognosis: Chalkbrood spreads quickly through the hive like a pandemic.

Treatment: Workers treat chalkbrood by tossing out dead larvae from the hive.

FOULBROOD, one of the nastiest and most tragic infectious diseases of a colony, is caused by a bacterium called *Paenibacillus larvae*.

Symptoms: Foulbrood earned its name from its characteristic awful smell. Larvae infected with foulbrood liquefy into a brown, smelly goop.

Prognosis: The comb's contact with the bacteria spreads the disease throughout the colony, infecting the brood who come in contact with it.

Treatment: There's no curing foulbrood, except with fire. Beekeepers must immediately torch the colony, and use propane to kill any remnant of the disease.

VARROA MITES appear as little red dots that latch onto the back of a bee: tiny mites that scuttle through a hive and spend their existence sucking a bee dry of its *hemolymph* (a bee's blood fluid). Varroa mites account for the most deaths in a colony.

Symptoms: Tiny red mites will appear on a bee's back.

Prognosis: A slow production, along with wings that shrivel from voorosis, becomes a sweeping infestation of the colony.

Treatment: Chemical treatments are often critical to killing off Varroa mites. Or using a breed of bee that has Africanized honey bee genetics.

23

KEEP AFRICANIZED BEES— AT YOUR OWN RISK!

Also known sensationally and misleadingly as "killer bees," Africanized bees are excellent pollinators, but often too aggressive to keep in a suburban or urban setting. Africanized bees also fly by the beat of their own wings; they do not keep well in boxes, and abscond into territories that best suit their hive.

24

HELP A BEEKEEPER PREPARE HIS OR HER HIVES FOR WINTER.

Winter, as we learned with gardening for bees, is the cruelest month. And commercial beekeepers have been experiencing up to 40% of their hives dying off in the winter. Help a beekeeper batten down the hatches of his or her brood, and learn along the way about winterizing a hive.

25

KEEP A LAB JOURNAL OF YOUR BEES.

Every great idea in science begins with an observation. Take down field notes and observations as you would a journal, and record changes you see within the hive.

26

LEARN THE JARGON OF BEEKEEPERS.

Like any other specialized hobby, beekeeping involves a blend of botanical, biological and sometimes just wonky slang terms. Here are some examples:

ABSCONDING SWARM: A mass exodus of an entire colony of bees due to disease, pests or other nest problems

BROOD: Bees that are still eggs, larvae or pupae

DEXTROSE: Also known as glucose; one of the two principle sugars in honey and has a tendency to granulate

FOOD CHAMBER: A section of the hive devoted to winter food stores

GRANULATION: The formation of crystals within honey

NECTAR: Sweet liquid secreted by nectaries of plants

NUCLEUS: A small hive of bees that cover two to five frames; the nucleus starts a new colony from scratch, rearing a queen, workers and drones

PIPING: A series of announcement sounds made by the queen before emerging from her cell

POLLEN: Male reproductive cell bodies of flower anthers

SMOKER: Device in which woodchips and burlap are burned to create smoke, which sedates the bees

Field Notes:
Banning Neonicotinoids

Neonicotinoids, or **neonics** for short, are insecticides chemically similar to nicotine and play a major role in the downfall of honey bees and pollinators worldwide. The effects of neonics on honey bees in particular have been well documented. Pesticides with neonics attack a honey bee's central nervous system, disorienting worker bees who come in contact with a tainted flower. Since the EPA reviews pesticides every fifteen years, the next review of neonics will come up in 2018. In 2013, the European Union outlawed four major pesticides that contained neonicotinoids, yet the US government is still slow in the pursuit to end usage of this devastating chemical.

Ever wonder how honey bee colonies differentiate between each other? Each hive has a unique odor for members' identification, almost like an ID card.

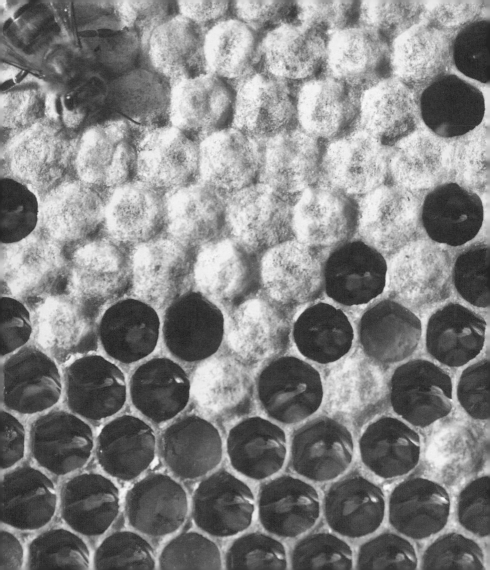

CHAPTER FOUR

CREATING, CRAFTING AND COOKING

Honey bees aren't all about making honey. Wax, royal jelly, bee bread and propolis account for just some of the dozens of different products created by the amazing honey bee. The process of harvesting these products, called "robbing the bees," is as rueful of an act as the phrase suggests. The process requires the keeper to invade a hive under a haze of smoke, which sedates the bees (while using smoke, you can even brush a bee's hairy back with a gloved finger).

With the lid open and the bees drowsy, the keeper proceeds to pillage the hive, removing each frame and, with a knife, cutting into the waxy comb to extract the goods.

27

USE PROPOLIS FOR RESINS.

Also known as bee glue, **propolis**' complex characteristics are due in part to its 50% composition of resins and vegetable balsams, along with a mixture of essential oils and wax. For ages, propolis has been used for its antiseptic and anti-microbial properties—think nature's bandage *and* antibiotic.

28 DON'T BUY THE BEAR.

Who doesn't love the iconic bear bottle of "honey"? After all, whenever we squeeze the contents of a generic honey bottle into our tea or onto our toast, we're reminded of a certain cartoon bear's heavy-handed blundering into a beehive or honey pot to scoop a paw-full into his mouth. However, these bottles of generic, non-local honey often consist of mere honey-flavored high-fructose corn syrup (HFCS). In other words, the honey is more likely the product of processed GMO corn than the natural product of a bee's harvest. Furthermore, generic honey often contains little-to-no pollen content.

It's no wonder you've seen those bears everywhere in supermarkets—the high-fructose corn syrup preserves the honey until the end of time! The studies conducted on HFCS have revealed myriad health problems. Hypertension, plaque buildup in arteries, diabetes, obesity—these ailments and disorders are a direct result of having a chronic diet of HFCS.

29 KNOW THE REWARDS OF REAL HONEY.

There are just no substitutes. Choosing generic honey over real, organic honey bottled by local beekeepers is like choosing a sack of pyrite over a stack of gold bullion. The bodily benefits of consuming raw, organic honey range from immunity boosts to super food energy. Some of the many health and nutritional benefits include but are not limited to:

- Vitamins B2 and B6, as well as minerals like copper, manganese and iron
- Anti-viral and anti-fungal properties
- Powerful antioxidants that help boost immune function
- Allergy prevention
- Balances blood sugar levels
- Cough suppressant and throat soother

30
KNOW WHAT TO LOOK FOR IN HONEY.

When shopping for honey, keep in mind the differences between pasteurized and raw honey.

PASTEURIZED HONEY: The pasteurization processes ensures a product is sterilized of harmful microbes and foodborne diseases. At 161°F, honey is safest to eat without risking a yeast infection or a very rare case of botulism. However, this level of heat destroys the original taste, fragrance and crystallization of honey.

RAW HONEY: Separated, rich and highly viscous, raw honey and its living microbes are spared the pasteurization process. You might find particulates of wax or tiny clusters of pollen. Raw honey has been used for its antihistaminic properties, along with its fragrance and unrivaled taste.

31

MIND YOUR OWN BEESWAX.

Workable, waterproof and reusable: The amazing physical properties of wax allow worker bees to mold it in complex, hexagonal geometric shapes. And if a member of *A. mellifera* can use wax to craft the most Byzantine structures of beehives, why shouldn't a *H. sapien* try to take up the honey bee's trade? Turn the page for some of the many useful products you can make from wax on your own.

PRO TIP:

NEVER MELT WAX DIRECTLY IN A SAUCEPAN. Use a double boiler instead; double boilers allow better heat distribution and keep wax at a safe temperature.

LIP BALM

1 teaspoon honey

$1/2$ oz beeswax

4 oz olive oil

10-15 drops of vanilla or mint extract for flavor (optional)

HAIR POMADE & MOUSTACHE WAX

¹/₄ cup pure-harvested beeswax

1 cup coconut oil (high viscosity at room temperature)

8-10 drops of lavender, peppermint, rosemary, licorice or similar essential oils

Storage tin (a reused pomade tin will suffice)

EYE SHADOW

4 teaspoons of grated beeswax

1 teaspoon of shea butter

¹/₄ teaspoon tea tree oil

1¹/₄ teaspoons of vegetable glycerin

2 teaspoons of pigment powder in your favorite color

¹/₄ teaspoon of mica powder

32

INTRODUCE HONEYCOMB IN DELICIOUS WAYS.

These are just some of the endless uses for honeycomb in everyday meals and snacks.

- Try placing a thin slab of honeycomb over your bowl of morning oatmeal!
- Take the ordinary combo of baguette and brie, and sprinkle lovely little pieces of honeycomb for an elegant snack.
- Concoct the most absurdly spicy chili, only to add a nice textured tang with—you guessed it—honeycomb.

My personal favorite:
HONEYCOMB, CRANBERRY AND BRIE BREAKFAST BAGEL

1 sesame bagel
I slice of butter
2 teaspoon of cranberry jam
4 oz thinly sliced brie
1 teaspoon crushed honeycomb

Instructions: Heat for 15 minutes at 325 degrees. The honeycomb will caramelize over the brie like flecks of gold leaf. Then add raspberry jam as a reminder of the honey bee's hard work!

33

TRY YOUR HAND AT BREWING MEAD AND TEJ.

Aside from Irish whiskey, mead, a wine made from honey, has been the drink of choice for English professors. The mead halls of *Beowulf* flowed with the golden liquid, and Geoffrey Chaucer arguably found his inspiration from mead.

Tej, like mead, is so delicious that the Queen of Sheba, King Solomon and their wedding party made legendary use of its intoxicating delights. Also known as *mase* in Eritrea, tej is a traditional brew in Ethiopia. Brewers of tej will flavor with sundried gesho leaves, an herb that tastes similar to hops.

34

REUSE WAX FROM CANDLES.

Similar to the way bees reuse their wax to fortify their hives (see #19), you can use and re-use beeswax to fortify your own home. Caulking drafty spaces in your home with wax can lower the cost of your energy bill and reduce your carbon footprint.

35

CREATE A SMALL BUSINESS OF YOUR OWN that keeps bees healthy and working. Maybe you have a friend who beekeeps, or maybe you're a beekeeper already? Why not turn a profit while celebrating the contributions of your local colony? Plus, it's much more fun—and profitable—than running a lemonade stand.

Field Notes: Running on Honey

Everyone has experienced a *bonk:* a depletion of glycogen stores in your muscles and liver. You might experience a bonk when running through mile 22 in a marathon, or simply running on one hour of sleep before a stressful deadline. So what happens to your body when the bonk fairy pays you a visit? First, your vision begins to dim (a bit like blacking out) and your muscles begin to cramp and shake uncontrollably. Some ultra-marathon athletes have even experienced hallucinations!

Honey, a complex carbohydrate, is a delightful treatment for the bonk. Here's a nice concoction for any hiker, biker or runner to enjoy:

ORGANIC HONEY AND CHIA SEED ENERGY DRINK

1-liter water bottle (like a Nalgene)
Hot water
2 teaspoons of honey crystals
2 teaspoons of chia seeds
2 teaspoons of raw or pasteurized organic honey

Note: The hot water actives the chia seeds and dissolves the honey and crystals. Flavor this concoction with slices of fruit (bananas and honey make a perfect combo!).

How much fuel does honey have? A teaspoon of honey can fuel a bee once around the earth.

CHAPTER FIVE

Giving Back
to the Honey bees

With all the science devoted to apiology, beekeeping and colony collapse, we still only know fragments about the plight of the honey bee. Humans have spent at least 8,000 years harvesting from honey bees, and even with our mountains of scientific research devoted to members of the *Apis* genus, there's still so much we don't know. Some burning questions on every apiologist's, farmer's and beekeeper's mind: What is causing CCD? How does climate change play a part? And do honey bees interact adversely with GMO foods? Science is still catching up with these unanswered questions.

While we wait for new peer-reviewed studies of honey bee behavior and collapse, we can try to reach a consensus on how best we can *give back* to the honey bee. After all, consider how a single worker bee toils her life away until her wings fall off for that teaspoon of honey you've swirled into your Earl Grey tea! The least we can do is try to compensate the honey bees for their thankless jobs—even if they have zero concept of human currency.

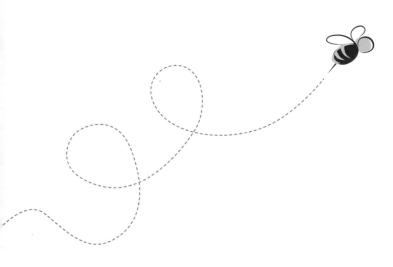

36

BEE A RESPONSIBLE CONSUMER.

Keeping bees alive means keeping bees in business. And the best way to give honey bees the job security they need to survive is to buy the produce they grow into fruition. We can save honey bees just by the way we shop the grocery store's produce aisle: seasonal, non-GMO, local and organic. Avoid fruits, vegetables and herbs grown with pesticides or other chemicals that harm populations of bees and contribute to colony collapse.

37

STUDY THE ECONOMICS OF BEES.

Earlier in this book, we took a crash course on botany and the honey bee's reason to *bee*, and we understand what honey bees adore about nearby flora. Now, we will explore ways to keep the bees doing what they love through the principles of natural supply and demand. The more we buy the products of bees, the more bees there are! Happily at work, season to season through nature's economics, bees give us the sweets and greens that make life fragrant and flavorful. There are ways we as consumers can not only keep bees employed, but also select with our wallets the right farms that grow their crops in the interest of pollinators.

38

SHARE AWARENESS VIDEOS ON SOCIAL MEDIA.

What if every viral cat video we watched had a social and ethical message attached to it? Short, hi-resolution documentaries devoted to honey bee conservation can be found on the Honeybee Conservancy's Website. And for every "Like" you receive, a new friend of the honey bee will be gained.

39

DISPEL THE MYTHS ABOUT HONEY BEES, PARTICULARLY THE AFRICANIZED BEE.

Some of the more pervasive myths involve this species of honey bees, and there have been waves of misinformation and fear that have unfairly characterized this important pollinator. Here are some facts to clear up the Africanized bee's maligned name:

- Africanized bees, contrary to their name, are a hybridization of the Western honey bee and other species of the *Apis* genus.

- Africanized bees are excellent producers of honey.

- Africanized bees are aggressive and should not be used in urban or suburban apiaries.

- Africanized bees are notorious absconders, and will leave a hive box in search of new nesting.

- Africanized bees are the best at fighting Varroa mites.

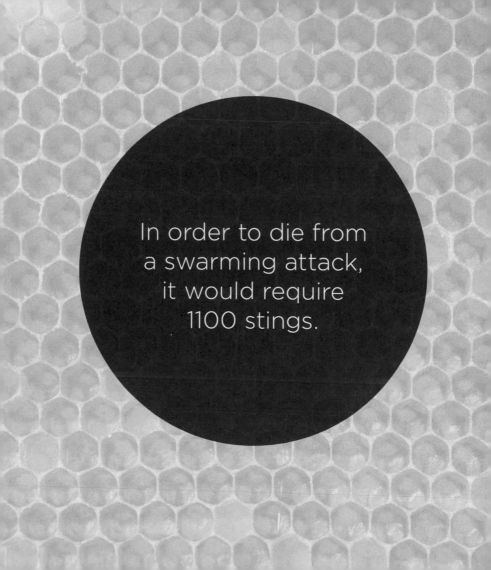

In order to die from
a swarming attack,
it would require
1100 stings.

40

AVOID FARMS THAT USE NEONICOTINOIDS.

You may recall neonicotinoids from the beekeeping chapter, and the destruction these pesticide chemicals wreak upon beehives. While it's difficult to point out the farms and produce companies who use this chemical, some nurseries that do not use neonicotinoids:

Digging Dog Nursery, Emersia Gardens, Eschraghi Nursery, EuroAmerican Propagators, Skagit Gardens, Terra Nova Nurseries, Walters Gardens, Xera Plants

41

VOLUNTEER WITH BEEKEEPING CHAPTERS.

Earlier in the book, we discussed joining a beekeeping group. If beekeeping and the act of getting your hands sticky doesn't appeal to you, perhaps you can help with driving! Apiaries are always looking for safe, reliable drivers to transport the precious cargo without incident. Helping with bottling honey, recycling wax or even building or repairing bee boxes can go a long way to make friends in the world of beekeeping.

42

DONATE TO HONEY BEE ORGANIZATIONS AND RESEARCHERS.

Established in 2009, The Honeybee Conservancy (http://thehoneybeeconservancy.org/) has been on the front lines, spreading awareness of waning honey bee health. A project of Social and Environmental Entrepreneurs, The Honeybee Conservancy spreads awareness in innovative ways through social media.

43

FIGHT FOR CONSERVATION AND SUSTAINABLE FARMING PRACTICES.

Conservation groups are at the forefront of fighting against climate change, pesticide policies and land grabs that could hurt the foraging habitats of pollinators.

SIERRA CLUB: Founded in 1892 by John Muir, the Sierra Club is both a conservation group and a team of brilliant environmental lawyers who recently played a large part in litigation against the EPA's approval of neonicotinoids.

350.ORG: Part of the goal of 350.org is to reduce the carbon footprint of the planet to 350 parts per million—a magic number that, backed by climate science, can slow and ultimately halt the progression of climate change.

POLLINATOR PARTNERSHIP (P2): Through funding conservation, education and research, the Pollinator Partnership advocates for pollinator health across the country. Since its founding in 1997, Pollinator Partnership has initiated programs like the North American Pollinator Protection Campaign as well as Pollinator Week designated by the U.S. Senate.

OTHER ORGANIZATIONS: Xerces Society, Million Pollinator Garden Challenge, The Honeybee Conservancy, HoneyLove and The Bee Girl.

44

SPONSOR
A HIVE.

If beekeeping isn't your cup of mead, "adopting" a beehive (much like adopting a highway) allows a caring person to purchase a beehive and leave it to a professional beekeeper.

45

REDUCE YOUR CARBON FOOTPRINT.

A study by University of Southampton suggests that air pollution from car exhaust contributes to mid-flight confusion in honey bees and other pollinators. Scent, along with ultraviolet light and electromagnetism, helps guide the honey bee to a flowering plant. However, car exhaust fumes mask the attractive odor of flowering plants. There are thousands of ways to reduce your daily carbon footprint—using solar energy, commuting via bicycle or driving electric. Finding clean, 21st century ways to fuel our lifestyle is the key.

46

GO VEGAN!

Maybe eating the byproducts of animals isn't your thing. And maybe the idea of robbing bees of their honey and wax unsettles you. There are vegan ways to keep honey bees in business without robbing them of their products. Following the tenants of a vegan lifestyle, like buying exclusively local and organic produce while abstaining from non-organic fruits and veggies potentially sprayed by pesticides, vegans do their part to ethically employ the honey bee.

47 DON'T BE AFRAID OF THE BEES.

Bees can be a nuisance—after all, those tiny barbs in the stinger can pack a wallop! Especially if you are one of the two million people in the US who have allergic reactions to stinging insects, apiophobia (fear of bees) is a rational fear to have. However, as much as bee stings have the potential to be deadly, we must understand the life-giving potential of a stinger's chemical makeup. For example, did you know the venom in a bee sting has been used in treatments to kill the HIV virus? A study conducted by the Washington University School of Medicine in St. Louis used nanoparticles found in bee venom to destroy the virus without harming surrounding cells.

48 RAISE A GRASSROOTS CAMPAIGN AGAINST NEONICOTINOIDS.

If the European Union can ban neonics in pesticides, why can't we in the US? One of the most effective ways to have your voice heard by your government is to create a viral petition. For a petition to be acknowledged by the President, 100,000 signees must be represented. Here are some useful facts about neonics to fuel change:

1. Neonics in pesticides are intended to be used to control aphids and grubs. However, the neonic chemicals are easily transmitted to pollinators when they contact a flower anther. Consequentially, honey bees, along with bumblebees and other pollinators, experience nerve damage caused by these contaminated flowers.

2. When a bee makes contact with a neonic, the neonic interfere with navigation components of honey bees.

3. Neonicotinoids not only contribute to CCD, but also contaminate entire ecosystems. Neonics pervade soil kicked up into the atmosphere from machinery, and contaminate seeds and groundwater.

4. Considered to be the new DDT, neonics are actually 7,000 times more concentrated than DDT content used in pesticides (before its widespread ban).

49

REGISTER TO VOTE!

If environmental issues are important to you as a voter, then pick the members of government who intend to work in the interests of our planet, and especially the honey bees.

50

LET CONGRESS KNOW WHAT YOU THINK.

Fighting for the honey bees means speaking up against the corporations like Bayer (the largest manufacturer of neonics) who lobby against regulations that could otherwise save our pollinators. Take the time to write a letter. And just to get the point across, mark the letter with a wax seal made from your own beeswax. After all, it's for them you're fighting.

Additional Resources

BOOKS

DeVito, Dominique. *Beekeeping: A Primer on Starting & Keeping a Hive*. New York: Sterling, 2010.

McFarland, Rob and Chelsea McFarland. *Save the Bees with Natural Backyard Hives: The Easy and Treatment-Free Way to Attract and Keep Healthy Bees*. Salem, MA: Page Street Publishing, 2015.

Nordhaus, Hannah. *The Beekeeper's Lament: How One Man and Half a Billion Honey Bees Help Feed America*. New York: Harper Perennial, 2011.

Readicker-Henderson, E. *A Short History of the Honey Bee: Humans, Flowers, and Bees in the Eternal Chase for Honey*. Portland, OR: Timber Press, 2009.

WEBSITES

HoneyLove
Honeylove.org

The Honeybee Conservancy
thehoneybeeconservancy.org

United States Environmental Protection Agency: Protecting Bees and Other Pollinator from Pesticides
www.epa.gov/pollinator protection

Photo Credits

The following images are used under official license from Shutterstock.com: 2, 7, 8, 14-15, 16, 22-23, 24, 29, 30, 33, 34, 36, 39, 40, 44, 47, 48, 51, 52, 55, 56-57, 58, 64, 66, 69, 70, 73, 76, 79, 82, 85, 87, 92-93, 94, 99, 100, 103, 106, 109, 110, 113, 114, 116, 118-119, 120, 123, 125, 126, 131, 133, 134, 137, 141, 142, 145, 146, 151, 152-153, 156-157

ABOUT THE AUTHOR

J Scott Donahue was a high school freshman in Mr. Hancock's English class when he first read Jon Krakauer's Into Thin Air. A decade later, he traveled to Nepal and wrote his Master's thesis composed of essays on travel and conservation. He contributes to Sierra magazine and YellowstonePark.com and finds wonder in climbing the high Sierra.

About Cider Mill Press Book Publishers

Good ideas ripen with time. From seed to harvest, Cider Mill Press brings fine reading, information, and entertainment together between the covers of its creatively crafted books. Our Cider Mill bears fruit twice a year, publishing a new crop of titles each spring and fall.

"Where Good Books Are Ready for Press"

Visit us on the Web at
www.cidermillpress.com
or write to us at
PO Box 454
Kennebunkport, Maine 04046